"Whether as a board mem
of Adobe, I have coached
mon's methods and leaders.
strongly recommend you add this book to your leadership library."

BRUCE CHIZEN; FORMER CEO, ADOBE SYSTEMS INCORPORATED [NASDAQ: ADBE];
ORACLE, BOARD OF DIRECTORS [NYSE: ORCL]

"Leadership matters. It can be learned if the aspiring executive is open to the process. 'One to Many' is not a magic curative, but rather a thoughtful guide to be used over and over throughout a career, not read just once and shelved."

STEPHEN LIGHT; CEO, XERIUM TECHNOLOGIES [NYSE: XRM];
FORMER CEO, FLOW INTERNATIONAL [NASDAQ: FLOW]

"I have worked with Chrismon for over a decade. This book hits the sweet spot – read the book, use the tools, become a better leader – simple."

THOMAS M. LINDQUIST; EVP AND COO; PLUM CREEK TIMBER [NYSE: PCL]

"There are literally thousands of leadership models and perspectives. In *The Shift From One to Many* Dr. Nofsinger drives quickly to the essential elements and delivers a brilliantly simple set of leadership tools and frameworks. This is a short read that packs a punch."

DR. STEWART I. DONALDSON; DEAN & CHAIR OF PSYCHOLOGY; SCHOOL OF
BEHAVIORAL & ORGANIZATIONAL SCIENCES AT CLAREMONT GRADUATE UNIVERSITY
[HOME TO THE PETER F. DRUCKER GRADUATE SCHOOL OF MANAGEMENT]

"The Shift leadership model is common sense made actionable – I use the tools daily; and find the concepts equally helpful in coaching my team."

DAVID FERINGA; VP OF SALES; F5 NETWORKS [NASDAQ:FFIV]

"I have guided hundreds of companies though strategic and go-to-market pro-cesses and in my experience it's quality leadership, more than any other factor, that is key in a successful execution. Chrismon cuts through the fluff and gets down to the essential with a simple yet powerful framework for a leader in any stage."

TOM KIPPOLA; MANAGING DIRECTOR; THE CHASM GROUP;
CO-AUTHOR OF THE BESTSELLING BOOK *THE GORILLA GAME*

CHRISMON NOFSINGER, PhD

THE SHIFT FROM
ONE TO
MANY

A PRACTICAL GUIDE to LEADERSHIP

LIVE OAK
BOOK COMPANY

Published by Live Oak Book Company
Austin, TX
www.liveoakbookcompany.com

Distributed by Live Oak Book Company

For ordering information or special discounts for bulk purchases,
please contact Live Oak Book Company at PO Box 91869, Austin,
TX 78709, 512.891.6100.

Design and composition by Greenleaf Book Group LLC
Cover design by Greenleaf Book Group LLC

Publisher's Cataloging-In-Publication Data
(Prepared by The Donohue Group, Inc.)
Nofsinger, Chrismon.
   The shift from one to many : a practical guide to leadership /
Chrismon Nofsinger. — 1st ed.
     p. ; cm.
   Issued also as an ebook.
   ISBN: 978-1-936909-08-7
   1. Leadership. 2. Industrial management. I. Title.
HD57.7 .N63 2011
658.4/092   2011935675

Print ISBN: 978-1-936909-08-7
eBook ISBN: 978-1-936909-09-4

First Edition

I dedicate this book to my family, and to leaders everywhere, that these tools might aid you on your career journey with ease, grace, and greater success.

CONTENTS

ACKNOWLEDGMENTS

It is with deep gratitude that I acknowledge the collaboration, encouragement, and support from many generous teams, organizations, and individuals who've joined me along the way.

The Nofsinger Group is indebted to hundreds of clients, executive teams, strategic partners, off-site participants, and students who have contributed to our thought processes. Without these valued partners and partnerships, there would be no insights, tools, or stories.

Finally, thank you to Alice Forsythe and Dana Questad for their wisdom, and to the team at Greenleaf Book Group, whose talent abounds.

INTRODUCTION

"If you want something done right, ask the busiest person in the room to do it."

We've all heard some version of this statement.

It suggests that if you are skilled, reliable, and deliver quality results, you will inevitably become one of your organization's "go-to" people and, often, will be promoted to positions of leadership.

But, despite abilities and achievements, many people frequently lack the knowledge, skills, and attitudes to perform well at their new level of responsibility.

This book is for those of you who, because of your skills and accomplishments, have been pushed to take on more. It offers tools to help you get up to speed more quickly and move into your new leadership role with ease, grace, and greater success.

CHAPTER 1

THE TRUTH ABOUT LEADERSHIP

We live in a culture that rewards individual accomplishment. Many of us are addicted to praise, or at least we expect some acknowledgment for our contributions. Every compliment, award, or bonus strokes our ego and makes us feel more valued, worthy, and confident.

This is natural. However, when we embark on a leadership journey, we need to realize that as the expectations of us increase, the rewarding strokes will become fewer and fewer. That's just the way it is.

You are probably reading this book because you've been thrust into a new role where you need to lead other people. You may have read a lot of books about leadership, each with its own definition of what good leadership entails. But here's the truth about leadership:

Leadership is about facilitating the output of others and giving them recognition.

That's it.

That's the secret sauce of leadership. All the requisite skills for leading people fall within that concept, and the good news is, those skills can be learned.

FACILITATING THE OUTPUT OF OTHERS

When we have a goal, we can either accomplish it ourselves or with the help of others. The former approach generally takes longer and requires more work. If you want to get something done, it is to your advantage to know how to lead others so they can help you accomplish your goal.

It doesn't matter if you're starting a new business or if you've been running a Fortune 100 firm for twenty-five years. It doesn't matter if you're coaching your child's Little League team or setting up a farmers' market in your community. To succeed, you need to learn to think in terms of what other people are capable of and what they need in order to feel valued—rather than in terms of your own abilities and your own needs.

This is a short book because the leadership concepts I outline here aren't really that difficult to understand. The challenge—and yes, there is a challenge or I wouldn't need to write this book—is human nature.

We are born thinking about "me." It's a survival thing. We think about our personal needs, like food and safety. As we gain in years and life experience, we think about our own talents and abilities, about finding our place in the world, and about earning money and building our relationships. It's all about me—what I need to do to get what I want.

The leadership journey requires that we shift from thinking first about ourselves to thinking first about others and their part in any effort in which we are involved.

GIVING RECOGNITION TO OTHERS

The other factor that predicts our level of effectiveness as a leader is our ability to suspend our need for recognition. We must train ourselves to recognize and acknowledge the accomplishments and talents of others.

I've interviewed and coached thousands of professional people and have discovered that the most successful are those who are willing to relinquish the need to take credit for everything they do. Simply put, successful leaders are great at giving credit to others. They have minimal need for personal recognition.

At this point, you might be inclined to defend your right to acknowledgment: "But I want all the credit for the work I do!"

Of course you do. There's nothing wrong with wanting or receiving acknowledgment. This feeling is natural. Babies cry to get attention. Children strive to excel in school, sports, and music to get attention. Adults work long hours and take risks to gain recognition and promotions.

But relinquishing the need for personal recognition is essential if you want to become an effective leader and attract quality people to work with you. The inability to acquire this one skill trips up many people who have been promoted into leadership roles. Their continuing hunger for praise, attention, and credit preoccupies their thoughts and guides their actions. As a result, they are unable to focus on facilitating the output of others.

If you accept that the skills and behaviors of leadership are learnable, you will find multiple opportunities to practice them every day. And the more you practice them, the more natural they will become.

CHAPTER 2

THE LEADERSHIP CONTINUUM

The journey along the leadership continuum offers you an exciting opportunity to learn a great deal about yourself and how you relate to other people. If you follow it to the fourth and final stage discussed in this book, Transferring, you will have a degree of influence that you probably cannot imagine right now. Even if you don't reach that ultimate stage, you will find yourself viewing the world from a much more comprehensive and powerful point of view.

Even the first steps of this journey will give you incredible insight into your own behavior and how you interact with others. You will find yourself making choices based on values that have the potential to change your life for the better.

The following diagram depicts the four stages of the leadership journey.

FROM ONE TO MANY ™

The From ONE to MANY™ model outlines the key stages every leader will have the opportunity to navigate during his or her career. It describes the journey from individual contributor to facilitating the output of others–the essence of leadership. We refer to this process as "Making the Shift".

ME

- Self-focused
- High need for control
- High need for personal recognition
- Possesses high interest or skill level in a particular area
- Prefers to do things himself or herself

US

- Begins to collaborate and value others' input
- Capacity for personal output is maxed out
- Begins to talk less
- Begins to ask more questions
- Begins to give credit and recognition to others
- Begins to leverage process

LETTING GO

- Consistently seeks out "A" players as friends, teammates, and mentors
- Regularly asks questions and seeks out others' thoughts
- Delegates responsibilities and authority consistently
- Communicates expectations and holds others accountable
- Fully leverages systems and processes

TRANSFERRING

- Understands the strengths and weaknesses of each key other
- Spends 50% of the time intentionally developing others
- Listening skills are excellent
- Low need for personal credit
- Consistently gives credit to others
- Surrounded by "A" players

ONE ――――――――――――――――→ MANY

The first stage is what I call the Me Stage. Most of us start our careers at this stage as individual contributors. We bring specific skills, experience, or talents to particular tasks and are singularly focused on our personal output. We see the world in terms of our own self-interest, and we view events and people through that lens.

We pass through the Me Stage to reach the Us Stage, sometimes shifting back and forth between the two as situations arise. In the Us Stage, we have reached a level of expertise where other people look to us for answers. We have more responsibilities and need to work with others to meet those responsibilities. We are still involved in day-to-day tasks, but we may be leading a team. We claim both personal credit for our contributions and shared credit with other contributors.

In the third stage, Letting Go, our efforts are almost exclusively focused on facilitating the output of others. For the most part, we have detached ourselves from day-to-day activities; we focus on the big picture and work primarily behind the scenes. We still draw on skills that we learned in the Me and Us stages, and we may have some hands-on involvement when the situation warrants it. We relinquish most of our need for personal recognition and give credit to others for their accomplishments.

The ultimate stage of leadership is Transferring. People at this far end of the continuum provide their value almost exclusively by facilitating the output of others. They spend their days thinking about people rather than tasks, and they have almost completely relinquished the need for personal recognition. They share their expertise and insights—their "gold"—and lift others up to their own levels of success.

I'll be honest with you: Not many people make it to Transferring. Those who do are truly exceptional leaders. You don't have to reach this ideal level of leadership, though, in order to be successful. Most people who work to progress along the continuum will end up somewhere in the middle.

As you continue to read about these stages, you might find yourself chuckling as you recognize yourself or a coworker, or recall a situation that might have had a different outcome if you had known about these components of leadership earlier in your career.

My goal is not only to give you tools and methods to meet your leadership goals but also to make these tools easy to remember and easy to apply in your professional life. You'll find that the ride is both profitable as well as profoundly satisfying and fun. Start experimenting with these tools, and you will see your influence expand and your personal satisfaction increase.

CHAPTER 3

IT'S ALL ABOUT ME

We all start out in the Me Stage. As children, we are basically selfish and perceive the world as existing to support us personally. Other people's thoughts, wants, and needs are not on our radar. As we grow into adulthood, we tend to temper this viewpoint and learn to view the world with a more expansive eye.

Many people operate in the Me mode for much of their lives, however, and the rest of us revert to it in certain situations, whatever our age or job title. We might be the president of a company or a salesperson. We might be a doctor or a data processor. Even as we acquire more leadership skills and progress along the continuum, we never fully leave behind the behaviors of the earlier stages because acquiring leadership skills is not a strictly linear process.

FROM ONE TO MANY ™

The From ONE to MANY™ model outlines the key stages every leader will have the opportunity to navigate during his or her career. It describes the journey from individual contributor to facilitating the output of others—the essence of leadership. We refer to this process as "Making the Shift".

ME

- **Self-focused**
- **High need for control**
- **High need for personal recognition**
- **Possesses high interest or skill level in a particular area**
- **Prefers to do things himself or herself**

US

- Begins to collaborate and value others' input
- Capacity for personal output is maxed out
- Begins to talk less
- Begins to ask more questions
- Begins to give credit and recognition to others
- Begins to leverage process

LETTING GO

- Consistently seeks out "A" players as friends, team-mates, and mentors
- Regularly asks questions and seeks out others' thoughts
- Delegates responsibilities and authority consistently
- Communicates expecta-tions and holds others accountable
- Fully leverages systems and processes

TRANSFERRING

- Understands the strengths and weaknesses of each key other
- Spends 50% of the time intentionally developing others
- Listening skills are excellent
- Low need for personal credit
- Consistently gives credit to others
- Surrounded by "A" players

ONE $\longrightarrow$ MANY

THE ME FILTER

In the Me Stage, when we're good at something, we seek recognition. Being the master of a certain skill is how we make
money, gain our self-worth, and define ourselves. What we're
good at can vary—it can be athletics, relationships, academics,
or some other pursuit or talent.

In the Me Stage, we view everything about our job—the
work environment, the tools and equipment available to us,
and the people around us—through a Me filter. Anything
that enhances or disrupts our ability to do our job seems
significant.

Let's say I have a favorite way of using e-mail to contact
sales leads and organize my sales efforts. Then the e-mail system is changed, and I have to adjust how I go about my work.
If this change helps me sell more products and communicate
better with my customers, I will probably welcome it. But if
it disrupts my way of doing things, doesn't help me do my
job, or interferes with my ability to meet my quotas, I will be
irritated and might complain to my boss. Why? Because the
new e-mail system affects me and my ability to do my job.

I'm not thinking about all the other departments and all the
other people who need to use the e-mail system, and whether
the change might in fact be beneficial for them. I'm only
thinking about how it affects my work. That's Me thinking.

CHARACTERISTICS OF THE ME STAGE

Each leadership stage has its own particular mode of self-talk, external language, and behavior or actions. Knowing these characteristics can help you identify what stage you are in and locate where other people in your life are on the continuum.

People with a Me focus are concerned about knowing exactly what is expected of them. Clearly defined benchmarks make it easy for them to gain acknowledgment, both from others and from themselves. They want to make sure everyone knows about their accomplishments, and they want all the credit for what they do. These people often use to-do lists as a vehicle for self-acknowledgment, and some even add easy tasks to their lists so they can check them off and enjoy that extra sense of accomplishment.

These people also want to do things the right way, and preferably the way they've been done in the past so they can't be blamed for coming up with a poor plan. This "follower" behavior helps them avoid mistakes and meet benchmarks in an approved manner that will likely earn them recognition.

We find martyrs of all types in the Me Stage. When they are overworked or overwhelmed, they do not suffer in silence. They make sure others know how hard they are working. They want acknowledgment for overcoming obstacles and life's challenges. People in this stage may even complicate their own lives just so they have more to overcome—and thus earn even more acknowledgment for their courage and capabilities.

In this stage, people tend to micromanage; they sometimes focus more on how something is done than on the desired outcome. I am not referring to the kind of control and precise methodology needed in journeyman professions. Obviously, electricians must wire a house according to specific procedures and abide by industry standards. Nor am I talking about such professionals as surgeons or pilots, who must follow specific steps in their work. I am talking about a need for control that unnecessarily avoids deviation or outside input.

This fixation on control can lead to the repetition of past inefficiencies or past mistakes simply because things have "always been done a certain way." It can also prevent people from taking advantage of improvements in technology and can significantly delay adaptation to changes in company goals.

LANGUAGE OF THE ME STAGE

The word "I" is central to the Me stage. We say, "I launched a new product" or "I led the creation of this group." The "I" symbolizes ownership and serves as a way of expressing accomplishment. In this stage, we don't talk much about other people, in part because we are totally focused on getting the clarity we need to do our job, and in part because everything and everyone else is off our radar.

For example, at my consulting firm, the Nofsinger Group, we worked with a first-time CEO whom I'll call Lillian. Lillian was fifty years old when we first met her. Despite her many years in management, Lillian was stuck in the Me Stage. She talked only about herself, and in meetings, she focused exclusively on her own ideas. As a result, her company was not as productive or successful as it had the potential to be.

You'll frequently notice an absence of "we" in the language of people in the Me Stage. Most often, they don't even mention other people's names.

As people progress through the leadership stages, they talk more about other people. They use names and describe others with some specificity, and they acknowledge other people's value. "Alexander really got the client on board—the project would have been toast without his efforts."

BEHAVIOR OF THE ME STAGE

Interestingly, just as we crave credit and recognition in the Me Stage, we also take on too much responsibility in order to achieve that outcome. When things don't go as expected, we're too hard on ourselves. Not only do we inflate the value of our contributions, we also take on too much of the blame.

A person in this stage will say, "If I had just made that last shot, we would have won the game," or, "I lost the state basketball championship today." This won't be objectively true, but it's how things look to that person. Other people might have botched passes or taken bad shots, but the person in the Me Stage assumes all responsibility for the failure, just as they would want all the credit for a success.

This feeling of ownership can be good in many ways. It makes people willing to work hard and get better at what they do. It might push them to become the top salesperson, the lead production engineer, or the star ball player. Many people do very well in the Me Stage for their entire careers and never realize or care that this egocentric behavior has kept them from moving to another level of accomplishment or leadership.

This lack of objectivity and overestimation of their own role leads people to appear uninterested in what others are saying. And they are uninterested. They don't listen. And since they can't listen, they bring very little creative thinking to team problem solving.

Problem solving requires looking at a situation from many angles to find the cause of the trouble. When you're in the Me mode, you can't get past your own contribution, your own part in the failure, or your own set of assumptions about the problem. You are limited to your own input.

MOVING BEYOND THE ME STAGE

What's interesting about the Me Stage is that as we become better and better at our jobs, we get busier and busier. We are awarded more accounts and more responsibilities, and we learn to become more efficient. And as we get more stuff done, we are given more tasks to do, and thus more opportunities for recognition. We feel like we are at the top of our game.

But, at some point, we can't handle it all. We get frustrated and stressed out because we have too much to do. We start to resent our boss and coworkers and feel anxious about our performance. Our workload exceeds our capacity. We feel taken for granted. We say things like, "I'm not a miracle worker, but if it weren't for me, they'd tank." We may complain about our heavy workload, but we may also sabotage efforts to relieve us of our work, and we may refuse help—because we're invested in our martyrdom.

In this situation, external circumstances can propel us toward the next leadership level. Either we're forced to accept help (e.g., our boss gives us an assistant), or we realize independently that we need to reach out to others for help with our workload.

Either way, we will have to team up and deal with other people, which can lead us into the Us Stage. As with the shift between any two leadership levels, this transition may last days, weeks, months, or even years.

CHAPTER 4

THINKING LIKE A TEAM

The second stage along the continuum, the Us Stage, is all about teaming up with others to get things done. In this stage, we realize that although we have many talents, we do not and cannot have every skill and talent needed to complete the work at hand. We must work with and value other people even though they may do things differently than we do and their skills may not be as polished in certain areas as ours.

My ten-year-old's soccer team is a great example of the dynamics of the Us Stage. Most of the kids are in the Me Stage, which is perfectly understandable. Each one thinks he is the most important player on the team. Each one thinks he is the starting forward, so they all run down the field kicking at the ball. Most of them don't pass; it wouldn't even occur to them to do so.

FROM ONE TO MANY ™

The From ONE to MANY™ model outlines the key stages every leader will have the opportunity to navigate during his or her career. It describes the journey from individual contributor to facilitating the output of others—the essence of leadership. We refer to this process as "Making the Shift".

ME

- Self-focused
- High need for control
- High need for personal recognition
- Possesses high interest or skill level in a particular area
- Prefers to do things himself or herself

US

- **Begins to collaborate and value others' input**
- **Capacity for personal output is maxed out**
- **Begins to talk less**
- **Begins to ask more questions**
- **Begins to give credit and recognition to others**
- **Begins to leverage process**

LETTING GO

- Consistently seeks out "A" players as friends, team-mates, and mentors
- Regularly asks questions and seeks out others' thoughts
- Delegates responsibilities and authority consistently
- Communicates expectations and holds others accountable
- Fully leverages systems and processes

TRANSFERRING

- Understands the strengths and weaknesses of each key other
- Spends 50% of the time intentionally developing others
- Listening skills are excellent
- Low need for personal credit
- Consistently gives credit to others
- Surrounded by "A" players

ONE ──────────────────────────→ MANY

When these young players start to move into the Us Stage, they become willing to say, "Okay, I play defense and you play offense." It's the beginning of understanding that there are roles and that in order to win, they need to play their designated roles instead of trying to be good at everything. They are learning to see other people's strengths and to accept that the assigned roles let all of the players use their particular strengths.

In the Us Stage, the players come to understand that it's not about their moment of individual glory but about the bigger picture. Although they don't realize it, these youngsters are beginning to apply the theory of synergy, which maintains that the collective performance of a team is much greater than the sum of the individual performances.

This is the same mind-set we must use when working with others to win that important account or that lucrative contract.

THE TEAM APPROACH

Over the past two decades, almost every reputable graduate program in business or related fields has moved from a model focused strictly on individual efforts toward one that is almost entirely team based. These schools recognize that in order for individuals to succeed in the highly team-oriented work world, they need exposure to and practice working in teams.

This shift in emphasis has proven its worth. In their eloquent classic, *The Wisdom of Teams*, Jon R. Katzenbach and Douglas K. Smith maintain that this team-focused, synergistic thinking has been a key ingredient in the continuous rise in productivity across all business sectors in the United States.

However, while teams can add a great deal of synergy to a project, they can also add challenges. Let's talk about the benefits first.

THE UPSIDE OF TEAMWORK

Synergy is what makes the whole greater than the sum of its parts. It's the energy and creativity that result when people can build off one another's ideas to come up with new approaches that none of them could have come up with on their own.

High-performance teams gain by working together, especially when their membership is diverse. The more diverse the team, the greater the array of approaches, perspectives, and skills.

Have you ever worked on or observed a team where trust was high, communication was good, and the team accomplished amazing things together? Through our firm, I've been fortunate to observe many such teams, through various assessment projects across the country and time in the field. Not only are these teams able to accomplish a lot; it's fun and satisfying to work with people in this way. Teamwork gives us all a deeper understanding of one another's knowledge, skills, and personal talents, which aids us in future collaborations.

THE DOWNSIDE OF TEAMWORK

An individual can make a single decision or a series of decisions relatively quickly because there is only one filter for deciding what needs to be done to reach a desired result. Working in a team setting often slows down this process. We call this process loss.

A handful of factors can slow down the process. First, the team has to make the time to work together. We all know how challenging it can be for busy people to clear their schedules. Then, we must allow time for people to gather the information they want to share. Collecting input from team members through brainstorming, while potentially very productive, can also be time-consuming. Meetings take time, and then we need more time to process the results of those meetings and come to conclusions.

Differing communication styles can also slow down the process. Everyone has a preferred method of communicating, receiving, and processing information. Analytical people talk about details. Controlling people talk about bottom-line results and want to cut to the chase. Supportive people want to know how everyone is affected. And the spark plug on the team wants to get started and figure out those pesky details later.

People also have different ways of filtering information, depending on their values, level and type of knowledge, skills, and talents. They will also use different methods to reach conclusions and make decisions.

CHARACTERISTICS OF THE US STAGE

In the Us Stage, we still do what we are good at and are concerned about doing our job correctly. But we are no longer doing that job as if in a vacuum. We solicit input from others. We go out of our way to facilitate cooperation. When we run a meeting, we ensure that everyone has an opportunity to contribute, and we might mediate between differing opinions. Our focus is on getting the team to work together to generate the best result.

In this stage, we respect what others have to offer, even when we think we have more knowledge or skill and can do the job better. Unlike in the Me Stage, where we are solely focused on getting recognition for our individual contributions, in the Us Stage we are equally interested in acknowledging the contributions of others.

LANGUAGE OF THE US STAGE

In the Us Stage, we use the word "we." But it is important to remember that "we" is still inclusive of "I." When I say, "We paddled down the river," it implies that I was in the raft and was a part of that journey. I'm still defining my contribution to the activity.

Creating and leading an effective team requires a level of maturity and some ego management skills. When people are willing to suppress their own egos and need for recognition in favor of acknowledging others, it allows for more trusting, respectful relationships.

This means letting go of total control and being willing to say, "I'm not sure I understand why this is the right approach, but the others seem convinced, so I'm going to trust them."

Shifting to the Us Stage also means stepping out of the limelight. We might say, "Sally is so much better than I am at dealing with the board, so I'll let her present and use my skills to crunch numbers for the report."

It means sharing recognition. Instead of saying to the boss, "Did you see that report I gave you?" we say, "Did you see the report we put together for you?"

It means recognizing our need for input and help. While we have been successful on our own, we are willing to share responsibilities and work with others. We say, "I can't do this alone. Fred is perfectly capable of doing this piece of the project without my input."

BEHAVIOR OF THE US STAGE

At this level, we are fully engaged in getting people to work together, actively soliciting input, and involving each team member in the process. The team members might still be in the Me Stage, with a need for clearly defined benchmarks and lots of recognition. We recognize those needs and work to get those needs met. This might include breaking down a project into specific tasks so each person has a clear idea of his or her role in the project.

At this stage, however, we will likely be very skilled at many of these same tasks and will want some acknowledgment for our part in the project. We will need to include ourselves in the "we" of the group.

We may become frustrated when others don't contribute or fully engage in the team effort. We may also feel frustrated if team members are reluctant to share the credit, and we may feel thwarted by a lack of cooperation, trust, and mutual respect within the team.

MOVING BEYOND THE US STAGE

Being a valuable contributor to a team is a perfectly acceptable career accomplishment, and many people are very successful and content working at this leadership level. That's great. We need good team players.

In the Us Stage, things might be going well. Our projects are humming along, we're reaching goals quickly, working well with others, and learning from the people we work with. We receive ample recognition for both our team's efforts and our individual efforts. But we're doing so well that we can hardly handle the amount of work we're getting, and we feel the pressure building.

We might feel overwhelmed, responsible for the outcome of the team effort, and frustrated when we don't get the cooperation we need or when someone doesn't perform up to standard.

We might think it's time to work at a higher level, where we can just tell people what to do instead of having to coddle them into cooperating. As the range and volume of our responsibilities grow, we eventually hit maximum capacity. We can't be all things to all people all the time. Something has to give.

Like the shift from the Me Stage to the Us Stage, the shift from the Us Stage to the next stage, Letting Go, is usually prompted by outside circumstances. The shift often begins when we get promoted, or when we reach maximum capacity and can no longer function at the same level. We shift from being a team player and sometime coach to being a full-time coach.

CHAPTER 5

THE POWER OF LETTING GO

The third stage, Letting Go, is where almost everything you do is related to recognizing the strengths and weaknesses of others, acknowledging their contributions, and giving them rewards and benefits for those contributions. You are not involved in the day-to-day activities of teams, and you are not interested in personal recognition.

The ability to move into the Letting Go stage does not depend on your age or what position you hold. You could be the CEO of a multinational conglomerate and still feel some need for personal recognition. In fact, the majority of business leaders never move entirely into the Letting Go stage.

Age and experience have little to do with the ability to move into this leadership stage. Take a twenty-six-year-old

FROM ONE TO MANY™

The From ONE to MANY™ model outlines the key stages every leader will have the opportunity to navigate during his or her career. It describes the journey from individual contributor to facilitating the output of others–the essence of leadership. We refer to this process as "Making the Shift".

TRANSFERRING

- Understands the strengths and weaknesses of each key other
- Spends 50% of the time intentionally developing others
- Listening skills are excellent
- Low need for personal credit
- Consistently gives credit to others
- Surrounded by "A" players

LETTING GO

- **Consistently seeks out "A" players as friends, teammates, and mentors**
- **Regularly asks questions and seeks out others' thoughts**
- **Delegates responsibilities and authority consistently**
- **Communicates expectations and holds others accountable**
- **Fully leverages systems and processes**

US

- Begins to collaborate and value others' input
- Capacity for personal output is maxed out
- Begins to talk less
- Begins to ask more questions
- Begins to give credit and recognition to others
- Begins to leverage process

ME

- Self-focused
- High need for control
- High need for personal recognition
- Possesses high interest or skill level in a particular area
- Prefers to do things himself or herself

ONE ———————————————→ MANY

running a software start-up, for example. This person might be very good at facilitating the output of others. He might even have what some would consider an intensive, hardcore, or demanding approach to driving results as his team pushes to proof of concept or seeks funding. In some organizations, this approach might be considered disruptive, but others need leaders who demand high performances not only from themselves but from everyone around them too.

We've seen high school students who are amazing leaders and who are already in the Letting Go Stage. They are successful captains of sports teams, heads of musical groups, and student body leaders. They understand the value of seeking out quality people, acknowledging their strengths, and giving them opportunities to exhibit those strengths and receive acknowledgment for them.

LOOKING THROUGH AN OBJECTIVE LENS

In the Letting Go Stage, we are much more objective about people, and we are focused on their particular skills and accomplishments rather than their likability. We are more objective about who can do the best work in a given role. This objectivity will earn us the influence to assemble a powerful team. Our team will perform well for us because they trust us to give them credit for their contributions. This will give us access to more power and increase our ability to get things done.

People who are able to see the bigger, more strategic picture rather than the day-to-day activities of specific projects talk about their hopes, their excitement, and their concerns as they pertain to outcomes. With this broader focus, they are much more accepting of ambiguity and everyday unknowns than are the leaders in the Me and Us stages.

LEARNING TO LET GO

Moving into a new leadership position doesn't automatically confer the next set of leadership skills, nor does it prepare you to start mastering those skills; therefore, you can expect some discomfort. As you progress along the continuum, you must leave certain behaviors and attitudes behind and acquire new ones.

As you transition to the Letting Go phase, you will feel some fear. I call this the "horror of letting go," and it is totally justified. You will no longer have your finger in every project, and you won't know everything that's going on, so you will sometimes feel out of control.

You will also sometimes feel that you are in over your head. You might think, "I can't do this. What made me think I could?" or, "What if someone messes up and I'm not there to fix it? The whole project could collapse. I know I hand-picked the team, but what if they screw up?" And screw up they will, at least once. It's not a matter of if, it's a matter of when. Handing over responsibility to others means trusting them to do the job. You must increase your tolerance for damage when they make mistakes.

CHARACTERISTICS OF THE LETTING GO STAGE

In the Me and Us stages, you might have been a very good engineer, and now you're in charge of several engineers and overseeing a major project. In your new role, what used to be your greatest strength is no longer relevant. Now your job is to be an ambassador and a shepherd for your team. Suddenly, being a top engineer isn't important. But if you are no longer the lead engineer, who are you?

When we step into a leadership role, we can lose our sense of identity—and many people are not willing to do that. Being a successful leader is less about having an identity and more about giving other people a sense of identity and purpose.

In the Me Stage, we got a lot done on our own. When we moved to the Us Stage, we learned to tolerate Me behavior in others, collaborate with a team, and give them credit. Now we are supervising people who are in the Me and Us stages. Not only must we tolerate egocentric behavior in others, we must actually facilitate their output and give them all of the credit, because that's what they need.

LANGUAGE OF THE LETTING GO STAGE

In the Letting Go Stage, we detach ourselves from the group and focus primarily on people and outcomes. We speak about our hope and excitement for people, but internally we must constantly wrestle with issues of fear, trust, failure, and loss.

A leader entering this stage might think, "All I can think about today is Jill and the meeting coming up on Thursday. She'll be there by herself, and she's handling the project well, but it's all I can do to restrain myself from attending the meeting, rewriting her e-mails, and calling the client to see how it's going. I don't know if it's because I don't trust her or if it's just my own need for control. It's just uncomfortable."

Over time, it becomes easier to trust, show respect for, and talk about the potential of specific individuals. The leader might instead think, "You know, Sean is getting things done. Melissa is getting things done. Luis is getting things done. They are doing a good job, and I'm able to work on some other stuff."

This state of being is a noticeable and profound change. When we are able to let go without our stomach churning, we've reached an important milestone in our leadership journey. The people who experience this shift can feel it. They know it intellectually too, but they can feel the shift and talk about it.

In the Us Stage, we use the words "we" and "us." In the Letting Go Stage, it's about "they" and "them." We don't even include ourselves. "They" did a fantastic job. We make a clear separation between ourselves and the team's activities and accomplishments. That is letting go.

BEHAVIOR OF THE LETTING GO STAGE

Letting go is an actual behavior that is both liberating and painful. The shift is hard, and it takes effort and self-discipline. As we become more effective as leaders, each progressive shift becomes harder and harder. It's like the difference between learning to be a good golfer and becoming a great golfer. It's much easier to go from golfing 110 to 100 than it is to go from golfing 100 to 90.

To enter the Letting Go Stage, we must relinquish some key behaviors that we are probably dearly attached to. This release will fly in the face of everything that has worked for us before. It's so difficult that few CEOs and managers ever make it to the Letting Go Stage—in my experience, less than 5 percent (without support or coaching).

Probably the biggest challenge is relinquishing the need for personal recognition. For many of us, this work-reward relationship has been a significant driver in our career progress and cannot be discounted as a motivation to excel. It can be extremely uncomfortable to give it up.

The fact is that in the Letting Go Stage, fewer and fewer people will acknowledge or appreciate us. That is one reason people retreat from this stage. Even leaders who do well at relinquishing their need for personal credit can fall back into Me and Us behaviors—by claiming personal credit after some time has passed, for example.

This is an understandable urge. It's hard to coach a team and not be able to claim some personal credit for their success. When we say things like, "I'm so glad Leslie and her team did well. I met with her and talked with her a few days before they launched the project," we are still looking for credit, however subtly.

The minute we say, "I told you it would work out" or claim credit for some success, we come down a notch in the eyes of the people we are leading—because it's no longer all about them, and it damages the trust we've built with them.

Still, claiming the credit later is better than doing it right away. If we slip up from time to time, it's okay. This stuff is hard.

To remain firmly in the Letting Go Stage, we would say something like, "Not only did Katherine do a good job, but I think we need to reward her for it." Excellence in leadership is giving all the credit away and even offering a tangible acknowledgment, such as a bonus, a trip, or an award.

Very few of us can do this consistently. Letting go is more subtle than whether we do it or not. It's how often we do it. And where. It may be easy to give credit to the chef who prepares an excellent meal because you can't cook and nothing is taken away from you by giving him all the credit. But it might be challenging to give credit to a colleague at work who tends to steal credit or criticizes or gossips about you.

So look at where you give recognition and credit. Look at how often you give it. Look at other areas in your life where you could give it more often and more consistently.

LEARNING TO LIVE WITH REJECTION

In the Letting Go Stage, the social aspects of your work life will also change, sometimes in uncomfortable ways. First, the more credit you give to others, the less they will value your contribution; people will start to think they don't need you and that you're dead weight. This can feel like a loss of respect from others.

Second, the more objective you become as a result of your new responsibilities, the more you will be perceived as aloof, an outsider. The better you become at remaining objective—matching the right people to the right jobs and holding others accountable—the more you will be perceived as disconnected and uncaring.

You are now the "other." You're the boss—someone to be wary of or someone who just isn't on board. You aren't perceived as part of the team anymore. This can feel like rejection from people you've known.

When I interview people and ask about someone who's in the Letting Go Stage, I often hear things like, "I don't think Paul really gets it. He's disconnected from what's going on. The team is doing the work. Two years ago, he was all over this stuff, but now he doesn't seem to care as much."

When you hear this kind of feedback, don't panic. Simply recognize it for what it is: a signal that you are doing your job.

The irony is that while you may appear more distant, you are anything but detached. You are invested in the success of the people you've chosen for these projects. You are doing everything you can to facilitate their output and ensure that they get recognition for their work. The aloofness that people perceive is actually your enhanced professionalism.

The beauty of this stage is that the people who recognize that there is a leadership transition under way will understand and appreciate the hidden work and dynamics in play. They will realize that you are associated with good outcomes all the time because you are facilitating the output of others, and that makes you a good leader.

Another social adjustment in the Letting Go Stage is that you do not base your success on whether others like you. You base your success on whether the people around you realize their potential. This detachment is really difficult. It can be lonely at the top.

MOVING BEYOND THE LETTING GO STAGE

The feelings of rejection you experience in the Letting Go Stage probably won't put you in the mood for Transferring, which is the next leadership level. It's hard to feel like sharing your most important insights and skills with people who seem to be showing you less respect. But that is exactly what the next level of leadership requires.

CHAPTER 6

GIVING AWAY THE GOLD

In the final stage along the leadership continuum, we spend more and more of our time looking for opportunities to transfer our wisdom to others. People who are good at this can often be spotted early on—they're the ones who, despite a commission sales structure, look over contracts or sales opportunities with more junior salespeople or brainstorm ideas that may benefit accounts in other divisions.

You can spot early signs of this behavior even at the individual contributor level. It's about giving away insights and ideas. Earlier in a person's career, the value of those thoughts and ideas may vary. But with the benefit of experience, the "gold" becomes more valuable and can often be delivered with fewer words but more impact.

FROM ONE TO MANY ™

The From ONE to MANY™ model outlines the key stages every leader will have the opportunity to navigate during his or her career. It describes the journey from individual contributor to facilitating the output of others—the essence of leadership. We refer to this process as "Making the Shift".

ME

- Self-focused
- High need for control
- High need for personal recognition
- Possesses high interest or skill level in a particular area
- Prefers to do things himself or herself

US

- Begins to collaborate and value others' input
- Capacity for personal output is maxed out
- Begins to talk less
- Begins to ask more questions
- Begins to give credit and recognition to others
- Begins to leverage process

LETTING GO

- Consistently seeks out "A" players as friends, teammates, and mentors
- Regularly asks questions and seeks out others' thoughts
- Delegates responsibilities and authority consistently
- Communicates expectations and holds others accountable
- Fully leverages systems and processes

TRANSFERRING

- Understands the strengths and weaknesses of each key other
- Spends 50% of the time intentionally developing others
- Listening skills are excellent
- Low need for personal credit
- Consistently gives credit to others
- Surrounded by "A" players

ONE ———————————————→ MANY

In the Transferring Stage, we are fully in the mode of delegating and letting go, as well as actively trying to understand people's strengths and weaknesses and to identify scenarios where we can pass along our knowledge.

A lot of people who are good at what they do find it difficult to enter this stage. It is easy to underestimate how much you know or to fail to recognize how many experiences and data points you have that can add up to insight. In this stage, you may share only one or two bits of wisdom so the other person can gradually piece together the whole picture independently. Describing the entire picture may or may not help them see it. What differentiates the truly effective leader is the ability to identify what to share and when.

You can see this natural tendency in some individuals regardless of their age. Some leaders, through some combination of learned and natural skill sets, are more effective and more comfortable when helping others develop. They naturally look for opportunities to promote the learning and growth of those around them.

For many, what gets in the way of giving away the gold is the impulse to say "I told you so." For instance, you've used your insight and experience to guide someone to a good outcome. But at some later point, you just can't help needing a piece of that acknowledgment. You bite your lip and clench your jaw, but you still can't resist saying, "Yeah, like I told you." Or, maybe over lunch with a third party, you say, "Well, he was almost there, but after I met with him he was able to figure it out."

We've all done this. But from a leadership perspective, we have to recognize these statements for what they are—overt bids for recognition. Keep in mind that we still get some recognition in this stage because our skills, experience, and insight will be sought after. But this stage is about not needing that recognition. Instead, we let the achievements of those around us speak most clearly about our own effectiveness and relevance.

At times, we might feel embarrassed or hesitant to talk about the way we really do things. For example, through experience a lot of executives have learned what not to do: what information not to ignore, what e-mails not to answer, and what events not to attend. Talking about our strategies out loud with a colleague or someone we're trying to help can feel too revealing, or feel like it will somehow diminish our credibility or reputation. But it's always worth taking that risk.

I have never met anyone who is good at giving away the gold who doesn't already have all the success he or she needs, financial or otherwise. The behavior of this stage is so uncommon that we don't see many role models for it. This makes it difficult to regard it as normal behavior.

CHARACTERISTICS OF THE TRANSFERRING STAGE

People enter this stage with all the characteristics associated with the Letting Go Stage. They are completely focused on facilitating the output of others and giving recognition. But as they move to this level, these characteristics take on a new depth. Not only do they constantly give credit; it is nearly impossible for them to accept credit for anything—they always find a way to deflect it toward someone else.

My firm has a few clients at this stage, and we will jump through any hoops for them because, over the years, through their words and actions, they have given us credit and recognition. They decide to hire us again, or they give us a referral or tell someone behind the scenes about us. They say to people, "You know, they really helped us." When someone gives you credit without reservation, it makes you want to continue doing an excellent job for them and for the people they refer you to. This is a very powerful influence.

Leaders in the Transferring Stage want others to be successful. By ensuring that other people succeed, they succeed.

They are willing to take the risk of sharing their secrets. This is actually a very small risk because not many people will actually pick up on what they are saying or understand its importance.

These leaders meet people where they are. They don't patronize or condescend. They convey their ideas in ways the recipient can comprehend based on their leadership level. But they actually listen more than they talk. They listen to learn what others need.

LANGUAGE OF THE TRANSFERRING STAGE

Leaders at this stage use vocabulary that will help people grow—whether it's a few people or hundreds of people. They refer to individuals by name, and to groups as "they" or "them" rather than "we" or "us." They connect with other decision makers in specific arenas. They talk about their own strengths and weaknesses, their approaches, and their efforts to connect to people.

They discuss how they can help others improve or expand their comfort level to gain more success. They talk about how they make decisions. They explain why something worked or didn't work. They share the inside scoop on how a deal was made, how a contract was won, or how an expansion was negotiated. They hold nothing back.

These leaders find endless ways to give credit, even when the credit is obviously theirs.

BEHAVIOR OF THE TRANSFERRING STAGE

Even in this stage, leaders may occasionally exhibit Me behaviors when a situation involves zero tolerance for error. If those planes must reach France by a certain time to deliver parts to your biggest client, you might need to take control; as much as you trust your foreman to get the job done, it needs to be your responsibility this time.

But normally we are not involved in the day-to-day activities of the people we are supervising. As I mentioned in the previous chapter, this can lead to feelings of rejection and resentment, or even a sense of betrayal when our elite team leaders begin to discount our contributions. We understand that we have deliberately created that distance, but it can still be hard to hear them say things like, "Hey, we're doing just fine without you."

Of the thousands of clients I have worked with, I can count on one hand the number of people who have made even a partial shift to the Transferring Stage. I wish there were more because we need more people to share their knowledge and raise others into leadership roles. Often, those who do make the shift do so only in certain areas of their lives. For example, a CEO who also coaches Little League may be ready to pass along his coaching insights to an up-and-coming coach but still hoard his gold in his professional life.

STRATEGIES FOR TRANSFERRING

Over time, we come up with ways to share our insights, strategies, and tricks of the trade with other people. Depending on the circumstances and the personalities involved, we might do this through a gentle suggestion or a forceful push. But we must always meet the other person where he or she is.

We may need to push someone to the edge in a challenging situation, tell her what she needs to know to manage the outcome, and then leave her to succeed or fail. We may intentionally push someone to his limit in order to help him gain an insight he wouldn't have found otherwise. I've employed these strategies and more in my role as an executive coach, an internal manager of people, and a thought-partner to executives in transition. The leadership tools available are many, but the end goal remains the same regardless of which strategy is employed.

You might drop little nuggets of wisdom where anyone can pick them up. I call this the "gum wrapper" strategy. Someone may pick it up on the same day or six months or five years later. It will be noticed when someone is ready to notice it. That might mean that of your seven direct reports, only two of them will pick up on the wisdom you share and under-stand its value.

The people who pick up on it might be two levels down. You'll notice that they are listening for your wisdom. These are high-potential people, and they're coming up at lightning speed. This process can help you identify these promising individuals and gain a serious edge when it comes to hiring new people or promoting coworkers to positions of leadership.

CHAPTER 7

PUTTING IT ALL TO WORK

We live in interesting times. All around us, systems are becoming too complex to function efficiently. We have too many regulations that are not enforced, too many laws that cripple business, and too many obstacles to becoming and staying healthy.

When systems become dysfunctional because they are too complex, they eventually collapse. This is called entropy, and we've seen it demonstrated throughout history. For example, when Roman laws became too absurd, the officials could not apply them. They became meaningless, yet still cumbersome. Eventually that system became dysfunctional and collapsed.

Today, we see entropy occurring all around the world. In the West, we've enjoyed decades of instant gratification and easy choices, and now it appears that political, social, and economic changes are taking place at an accelerated rate. Time is becoming compressed. We used to be able to sit on a decision for six months, or even five years. Now things have to be done in two to three weeks.

We no longer have the luxury of making these shifts into leadership slowly. More and more people are needed to step into leadership roles in some capacity and contribute something meaningful to the world.

TAKING OUR PLACE IN LEADERSHIP

In the developed world, we expect things to work. But who makes things work? Who are the leaders who take responsibility for making them work? Who is the mayor? Who is the governor? Who are the industry leaders?

Society requires leaders, yet fewer and fewer people want to take on the challenge. In these troubling times, fewer people want to take on the job of mayor or president of the United States or even CEO. Most people don't want these jobs because they don't want that level of responsibility and the pressure that accompanies such jobs.

Some of that pressure comes from the huge number of vocal stakeholders for every issue. With all this clamor, it is more and more difficult to get things done. That is why leadership is so critical.

THE LEADERSHIP JOURNEY IN THE WORKPLACE

Now that you understand the leadership journey and are familiar with the tools that can help you navigate it, you will find many circumstances where you can apply these tools, especially in the workplace.

You can use the leadership continuum as a road map for your own career, learning the behaviors that can keep you on course and looking out for potential obstacles and avoiding them. You can use this model to hire and promote with success, as well as define job responsibilities, set goals, build successful teams, and gain cooperation from others.

Understanding this model can give you a significant edge when it comes to forming partnerships and putting together teams, whether you're building a neighborhood soccer team or putting together a multimillion-dollar business enterprise. This model can also be a powerful stimulus for changing the culture within a company by increasing trust among your people and providing the right motivation for them to perform with excellence.

This leadership journey is not just for people who want financial gain from their efforts, although that is a fine goal and one that is necessary for healthy commerce. The tools presented in this book can be valuable in all areas of your life.

LEADERSHIP AT HOME AND IN THE COMMUNITY

You don't have to go to the workplace to put your new leadership skills to work. Maybe you'll spearhead a movement to save the Alaskan coastline from oil drilling. Or lead a lobbying effort to ensure that organic farms are funded through their start-up years. Or maybe you'll organize medical teams to provide disaster relief.

On a smaller scale, you can give a batting tip to your eight-year-old and then step back while he swings. You can practice parallel parking with your teenager until she can do it perfectly on her own.

There are hundreds of ways you can teach, encourage, or in some way facilitate the output of others so they can experience greater success. When you understand where people are in their own journeys and what they need to feel good about themselves and their performances, you will be more inclined to help them and less likely to feel excessive frustration.

These leadership skills will improve your life and your relationships. They will transform you into a person of influence who can make a difference in your community and in the world.

IT'S NOT EASY, BUT IT'S WORTH IT

The leadership journey is hard. It's hard not to want personal recognition for your work. It's hard to have people reject you when you move beyond daily ordinary tasks. And it's hard to give your best ideas away in order to facilitate the output of others. It's hard, but it's worth it.

I hope this book will inspire you to make conscious choices in your career and take this journey. You can make a critical difference in many people's lives when you move beyond your own need for personal recognition and focus instead on facilitating the output of others. It is immensely rewarding because you can see tangible evidence of your influence.

ABOUT THE AUTHOR

Chrismon Nofsinger is the CEO and founder of the Nofsinger Group, a management consulting firm focused on executive leadership assessment and development. For more than twenty years, Chrismon has served as a trusted confidant and advisor to numerous CEOs, board members, and private equity investors. He earned an MA and a PhD in organizational psychology from Claremont Graduate University, where he was a student of management guru Peter F. Drucker. Chrismon now serves as a board member for the University. A sought-after speaker and thought leader, Chrismon frequently speaks to business, academic, and nonprofit groups on the use of stage models as a tool to meaningfully improve business interactions and relationships. Chrismon lives in Seattle with his wife, Rena, and their two sons.